D1313869

LIVING WITH DISEASES AND DISORDERS

Asthma, Cystic Fibrosis, and Other Respiratory Disorders

LIVING WITH DISEASES AND DISORDERS

LIVING WITH DISEASES AND DISORDERS

ADHD and Other Behavior Disorders

Allergies and Other Immune System Disorders

Asthma, Cystic Fibrosis, and Other Respiratory Disorders

Autism and Other Developmental Disorders

Cancer and Sickle Cell Disorder

Cerebral Palsy and Other Traumatic Brain Injuries

Crohn's Disease and Other Digestive Disorders

Depression, Anxiety, and Bipolar Disorders

Diabetes and Other Endocrine Disorders

Migraines and Seizures

Muscular Dystrophy and Other Neuromuscular Disorders

LIVING WITH DISEASES AND DISORDERS

Asthma, Cystic Fibrosis, and Other Respiratory Disorders

CAROLE HAWKINS

SERIES ADVISOR

HEATHER L. PELLETIER, Ph.D.

Pediatric Psychologist, Hasbro Children's Hospital
Clinical Assistant Professor, Warren Alpert Medical School of Brown University

MASON CREST

Mason Crest
450 Parkway Drive, Suite D
Broomall, PA 19008
www.masoncrest.com

MTM Publishing, Inc.
435 West 23rd Street, #8C
New York, NY 10011
www.mtmpublishing.com

President: Valerie Tomaselli
Vice President, Book Development: Hilary Poole
Designer: Annemarie Redmond
Copyeditor: Peter Jaskowiak
Editorial Assistant: Leigh Eron

Series ISBN: 978-1-4222-3747-2
Hardback ISBN: 978-1-4222-3750-2
E-Book ISBN: 978-1-4222-8031-7

Library of Congress Cataloging-in-Publication Data
Names: Hawkins, Carole, author.
Title: Asthma, cystic fibrosis, and other respiratory disorders / by Carole Hawkins; Series Consultant: Heather Pelletier, PhD, Hasbro Children's Hospital, Alpert Medical School/ Brown University.
Description: Broomall, PA : Mason Crest, [2018] | Series: Living with diseases and disorders | Audience: Age: 12+ | Audience: Grade 7 to 8. | Includes index.
Identifiers: LCCN 2016053134 (print) | LCCN 2016053671 (ebook) | ISBN 9781422237502 (hardback : alk. paper) | ISBN 9781422280317 (ebook)
Subjects: LCSH: Respiratory organs—Diseases—Juvenile literature.
Classification: LCC RC731 .H39 2018 (print) | LCC RC731 (ebook) | DDC 616.2—dc23
LC record available at https://lccn.loc.gov/2016053134

Printed and bound in the United States of America.

First printing
9 8 7 6 5 4 3 2 1

QR CODES AND LINKS TO THIRD PARTY CONTENT

TABLE OF CONTENTS

Key Icons to Look for:

 Words to Understand: These words with their easy-to-understand definitions will increase the reader's understanding of the text, while building vocabulary skills.

 Sidebars: This boxed material within the main text allows readers to build knowledge, gain insights, explore possibilities, and broaden their perspectives by weaving together additional information to provide realistic and holistic perspectives.

 Educational Videos: Readers can view videos by scanning our QR codes, which will provide them with additional educational content to supplement the text. Examples include news coverage, moments in history, speeches, iconic sports moments, and much more.

 Text-Dependent Questions: These questions send the reader back to the text for more careful attention to the evidence presented there.

 Research Projects: Readers are pointed toward areas of further inquiry connected to each chapter. Suggestions are provided for projects that encourage deeper research and analysis.

 Series Glossary of Key Terms: This back-of-the-book glossary contains terminology used throughout the series. Words found here increase the reader's ability to read and comprehend higher-level books and articles in this field.

SERIES INTRODUCTION

According to the Chronic Disease Center at the Centers for Disease Control and Prevention, over 100 million Americans suffer from a chronic illness or medical condition. In other words, they have a health problem that lasts three months or more, affects their ability to perform normal activities, and requires frequent medical care and/or hospitalizations. Epidemiological studies suggest that between 15 and 18 million of those with chronic illness or medical conditions are children and adolescents. That's roughly one out of every four children in the United States.

These young people must exert more time and energy to complete the tasks their peers do with minimal thought. For example, kids with Crohn's disease, ulcerative colitis, or other digestive issues have to plan meals and snacks carefully, to make sure they are not eating food that could irritate their stomachs or cause pain and discomfort. People with cerebral palsy, muscular dystrophy, or other physical limitations associated with a medical condition may need help getting dressed, using the bathroom, or joining an activity in gym class. Those with cystic fibrosis, asthma, or epilepsy may have to avoid certain activities or environments altogether. ADHD and other behavior disorders require the individual to work harder to sustain the level of attention and focus necessary to keep up in school.

Living with a chronic illness or medical condition is not easy. Identifying a diagnosis and adjusting to the initial shock is only the beginning of a long journey. Medications, follow-up appointments and procedures, missed school or work, adjusting to treatment regimens, coping with uncertainty, and readjusting expectations are all hurdles one has to overcome in learning how to live one's best life. Naturally, feelings of sadness or anxiety may set in while learning how to make it all work. This is especially true for young people, who may reach a point in their medical journey when they have to rethink some of their original goals and life plans to better match their health reality.

Chances are, you know people who live this reality on a regular basis. It is important to remember that those affected by chronic illness are family members, neighbors, friends, or maybe even our own doctors. They are likely navigating the demands of the day a little differently, as they balance the specific accommodations necessary to manage their illness. But they have the same desire to be productive and included as those who are fortunate not to have a chronic illness.

This set provides valuable information about the most common childhood chronic illnesses, in language that is engaging and easy for students to grasp. Each chapter highlights important vocabulary words and offers text-dependent questions to help assess comprehension. Meanwhile, educational videos (available by scanning QR codes) and research projects help connect the text to the outside world.

Our mission with this set is twofold. First, the volumes provide a go-to source for information about chronic illness for young people who are living with particular conditions. Each volume in this set strives to provide reliable medical information and practical advice for living day-to-day with various challenges. Second, we hope these volumes will also help kids without chronic illness better understand and appreciate how people with health challenges live. After all, if one in four young people is managing a health condition, it's safe to assume that the majority of our youth already know someone with a chronic illness, whether they realize it or not.

With the growing presence of social media, bullying is easier than ever before. It's vital that young people take a moment to stop and think about how they are more similar to kids with health challenges than they are different. Poor understanding and low tolerance for individual differences are often the platforms for bullying and noninclusive behavior, both in person and online. Living with Diseases and Disorders strives to close the gap of misunderstanding.

The ultimate solution to the bullying problem is surely an increase in empathy. We hope these books will help readers better understand and appreciate not only the daily struggles of people living with chronic conditions, but their triumphs as well.

—Heather Pelletier, Ph.D.
Hasbro Children's Hospital
Warren Alpert Medical School of Brown University

WORDS TO UNDERSTAND

antibodies: substances produced by the body to fight disease.

chronic: an illness that continues for a long time or keeps coming back.

diaphragm: a flat muscle below the rib cage.

expel: to push or force something out.

inflammation: a condition in which a part of your body becomes red, swollen, and painful.

irritant: something that causes slight inflammation (such as in the lungs) or other discomfort.

membrane: a thin sheet of tissue that acts as a barrier.

microorganism: a living thing so small it can only be seen with a microscope.

mucus: a thick liquid produced in some parts of the body to moisten and protect.

nebulizer: a machine that turns liquid medicine into a fine mist that's inhaled into the lungs.

phlegm: mucus that comes from the airways and leaves the body by being coughed out.

respiratory: relating to breathing.

spasm: a sudden uncontrolled tightening of a muscle.

toxic: poisonous.

trigger: something that causes another thing to happen.

CHAPTER ONE

What Is Respiratory Disease?

How long can you hold your breath? Try it right now. It's easy for about 30 seconds. At around 45 seconds, though, you'll start feeling pressured. After a minute, your heart will start to pound. Breathing is so fundamental to life that we do it without thinking about it. But when breathing stops, it doesn't take long to notice. The average person can last for weeks without food, days without water, but only about three minutes without air.

When you breathe air, you use your body's **respiratory** system, which includes your mouth, nose, and lungs. None of the body's other systems can function without it. The respiratory system delivers the oxygen to your bloodstream that fuels every cell in your body. It also helps to remove your cells' carbon dioxide waste. When breathing stops, carbon dioxide reaches **toxic** levels in the bloodstream within minutes and causes death.

With so much at stake, it might be hard to imagine a life where simply taking in and using a breath of air is difficult. But that's the challenge people with **chronic** respiratory disease face every day.

What Does Respiratory Disease Feel Like?

If you've ever had a cold, you have a vague idea of what it feels like to live with a chronic respiratory disease. A cold is a mild respiratory disease caused by viruses. A virus plants itself in your airways, takes over healthy cells, and reproduces. Your body fights back, using **inflammation** to contain the invading virus, **antibodies** to kill it, and extra **mucus** to wash all of the diseased substances away. Unfortunately, these defenses can also make you uncomfortable. The inflammation narrows your airways, and the extra mucus clogs them. Your breath is wheezy and you cough. You feel run down and you may lose your appetite.

The average cold goes away on its own in about a week. On the other hand, chronic respiratory diseases last much longer—some are permanent, while others get better with time—and the symptoms are more serious. Chronic respiratory diseases can make breathing so difficult that people need medical treatments, which may include a **nebulizer** to clear their airways or an oxygen tank to supplement the oxygen they get from the air.

How a Healthy Respiratory System Works

In order to understand chronic respiratory diseases, we need to take a closer look at the respiratory system.

Your respiratory system is made up of your mouth and nose, lungs, and all the air passageways connecting them. Those passageways include nasal cavities, your throat, your windpipe, and a network of airways branching into your lungs

Everybody who has had a cold can imagine what respiratory disorders feel like.

called the bronchi. The bronchi look like upside down trees, where a tiny "trunk" divides into as many as 30,000 tiny "branches."

When you breathe, your **diaphragm** contracts, moving downward into your abdomen. The negative pressure sucks air into your lungs and expands them. The air reaches the bronchi's smallest branches, each of which end in a

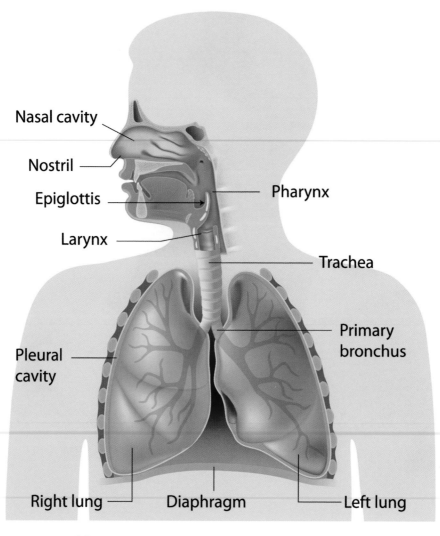

The major parts of the respiratory system.

bunch of inflatable air sacs, called alveoli. The alveoli's **membranes** are covered with tiny blood vessels. Oxygen crosses over the membranes into the blood stream, and the blood rushes to the parts of the body where oxygen is needed. Carbon dioxide, meanwhile, travels in the opposite direction: it passes out of the alveoli and is exhaled.

EDUCATIONAL VIDEO

Scan this code for a video about the respiratory system.

In addition to the oxygen we need to survive, the air we breathe also carries **microorganisms** and **irritants**, all of which can harm the body. To combat this, respiratory system airways are covered with sticky mucus and thousands of tiny hairs, called cilia. The microorganisms and pollutants get stuck in the mucus, and the cilia sweep the mucus back up the respiratory tract to be sneezed out, coughed up, or swallowed.

How Do Things Go Wrong?

When a person has a chronic respiratory disease, the body's air delivery system breaks down. This can happen if the air passageways become blocked, making it more difficult to get oxygen to alveoli and the tiny blood vessels. This is what happens when a person gets a serious respiratory infection, such as bronchitis or pneumonia. There's inflammation, and lot of fluid is produced that blocks bronchial tubes or fills the air sacs.

When a person has asthma, things like smoke or mold irritate the bronchial tubes and **trigger** the immune system. There's inflammation and mucus, just as

EARLY TREATMENTS FOR RESPIRATORY DISEASE

In the past, people knew far less about the causes and treatments of disease than we do now. Many early treatments for respiratory disease had no basis in science. Nevertheless, people sometimes stumbled across a remedy that relieved symptoms.

Coughs and colds were fought with teas made from herbs, wild cherry, or honey. They also were treated with aromatic substances, like menthol and eucalyptus. A few of these folk remedies were effective because they contained naturally occurring antihistamines, which are substances that reduce inflammation. Some helped in breaking down phlegm. Menthol was used to cool the pain of a sore throat.

In the 1700s, scientists came to understand that the respiratory system took in oxygen and expelled carbon dioxide. The discovery led the English physician Thomas Beddoes to test oxygen as a treatment for diseases like tuberculosis and asthma.

Another turning point in treating diseases came in the 1800s, when scientists came to understand how germs worked. They realized that some microorganisms could be used to kill other microorganisms, a discovery that paved the way for developing vaccines to fight infections.

there is with an infection. But there can also be muscle spasms in the bronchi, which can leave a person gasping for breath.

Another way your body's air delivery system can break down is if the lung tissues themselves become damaged and don't work properly. This happens, for example, with a respiratory disease called chronic obstructive pulmonary disorder (COPD; see chapter four). The alveoli get stiff and baggy and some of them break; this usually occurs after years of smoking cigarettes.

A World with Better Breathing

Some respiratory diseases mainly affect older people, like COPD. Others affect young people, too. According to the Centers for Disease Control and Prevention

A young woman in Beijing, China, wears a mask to try and protect herself from air pollution.

POLLUTION AND BREATHING PROBLEMS

Does cleaner air mean better breathing? New research shows it probably does.

An area once famous for its smog, today California has tougher standards for vehicle exhaust and has worked to rein in pollution from its seaports. The efforts seem to have worked. When scientists studied eight communities near Los Angeles, they found fewer reports of bronchitis, congestion, and chronic coughs among children than reported 20 years ago.

Air pollution has been recognized by governments as a threat to respiratory health for a long time. The city of Pittsburgh, Pennsylvania, adopted laws in 1815 restricting the amount of smoke a chimney could put into the air. Chicago and Cincinnati soon followed with similar laws. In 1948 in Donora, Pennsylvania, half of the town's people became sick, and 20 died, when fog and weather conditions caused pollution from the town's steel mills to become trapped over the town. A similar five-day fog covered London in 1952. Known as the Great London Smog, it was believed to have caused the deaths of about 4,000 people.

(CDC), more than 24 million Americans suffer from asthma. Of those, more than 6 million are children and teenagers. Meanwhile, about 1,000 people per year in the United States are diagnosed with a disorder called cystic fibrosis (CF). CF affects not only the respiratory system but also digestion, and symptoms typically appear at a very young age.

Some respiratory problems are preventable, while others are not. You can lower your chances of getting sick from things like flu and pneumonia by getting vaccinated, washing your hands often, and getting regular medical checkups. Your chances of developing COPD will be much lower if you don't smoke.

On the other hand, it's not clear how to prevent asthma. But if you have asthma, there are things you can do to make your symptoms less severe. You can take medicine prescribed by your doctor, and do your best to avoid things that trigger an attack. That might mean staying indoors on days when pollen counts are high, keeping away from pets, or leaving an area where people are smoking cigarettes.

Text-Dependent Questions

1. What does the respiratory system do?
2. How do diseases make it hard for the respiratory system to work properly?
3. What are some of the ways people get respiratory disease?

Research Project

Find out how many people in your county have asthma, COPD, and lung cancer by going to the American Lung Association's web page on the estimated prevalence and incidence of lung disease at www.lung.org/our-initiatives/research/monitoring-trends-in-lung-disease/estimated-prevalence-and-incidence-of-lung-disease. Compare rates of asthma in your county to two or three other counties, picking both rural and urban counties. (Hint: They will be easier to compare if you use Total Population to calculate percentages.) How does your county compare to the others? What factors do you think are responsible for the differences? You can look at a website like City-Data.com to find out median age, income, and types of jobs for the different counties to help you decide.

WORDS TO UNDERSTAND

disparity: a noticeable difference.

epidemic: when a disease spreads very quickly and affects a large number of people.

genetics: the scientific study of inherited traits.

proactive: taking an action to solve a problem *before* the problem starts.

stimulant: a drug that gives you more energy.

thermal: designed to keep you warm or cool by preventing heat from passing through.

CHAPTER TWO

Asthma

Imagine lying underwater and trying to take breaths of air from the surface through a thin straw. You may gasp for air, or you may take a lot of quick, shallow, breaths. But no matter what you try, you'll feel like you aren't getting nearly as much air as you need. This is a bit what it feels like to have an asthma attack.

Asthma is a chronic disease that affects the bronchial airways in the lungs. The airways become inflamed, which makes them oversensitive. When exposed to irritants, the airways narrow. This makes it harder to breathe, and you may wheeze and cough.

We don't know exactly why some people develop asthma and others do not. Researchers believe the condition is likely caused by a blend of genetic and environmental factors. An asthma attack can be triggered by many different things, such as allergies, dust, and cigarette smoke. A large amount of physical activity can sometimes also bring on an asthma attack. But not everyone gets an asthma attack from the same things. That has made it difficult for researchers to understand what exactly causes asthma, and it's also one of the reasons why there's still no cure for it. Instead of seeking a cure, people with asthma learn to manage their symptoms.

A doctor can diagnose asthma based on a physical exam and some specific asthma tests.

They take medicine—often carrying a device called an "inhaler" everywhere they go—and they also try to avoid things that could trigger an attack.

Asthma is linked to air pollution and dense urban living. This is one reason why it has become more common in the contemporary world. It has also become a serious health issue in recent decades. The number of children in the United States diagnosed with asthma doubled between 1980 and 1995, causing some researchers to declare an asthma epidemic. Then the growth leveled off. Researchers think the sharp increase might have been due in part to doctors becoming more aware of asthma in their young patients—in other words, there were more kids with asthma because more kids were being diagnosed. Today, asthma is one of the most common chronic childhood diseases.

What Are Asthma Triggers?

Asthma affects different people differently. Not everybody with asthma has attacks. For some people, asthma might take the form of a tickling cough after exercise. Or asthma might cause someone to wake up frequently at night from coughing. Whatever type of asthma you have, your symptoms are caused by substances that irritate the airways in your lungs. These irritants are called triggers. Not everyone with asthma has the same triggers, but there are a number of common ones.

Allergens. If you have asthma, you might get wheezy from pollen, your friend's cat, or mold from damp places in your house. Small particles from cockroach droppings can also set off an attack, as can droppings from

EDUCATIONAL VIDEO

Scan this code for a video about the causes of asthma.

Cat dander does not cause asthma, but it is common for people with asthma to also have pet allergies.

house dust mites, creatures so small they can only be seen with a microscope. Unfortunately, dust mites live in every house—on beds, pillows, and blankets, and even on stuffed animals.

Allergies do not cause asthma, but the two problems are related. Interestingly, the connection between allergies and asthma goes beyond obvious triggers like pollen. About 60 percent of people with asthma are also allergic to something, according to the Asthma and Allergy Foundation of America. The allergens don't have to be airborne—a certain food could actually be an asthma trigger for some people.

If you have allergic asthma, you will need to treat both conditions. Getting allergy shots gradually builds up a tolerance to triggers, so your body no longer overreacts to them. That in turn can help reduce asthma attacks. You can also take medicine before you have a reaction. For example, sometimes people need to use an inhaler after eating certain foods. Others may start taking allergy medicine in a proactive way—meaning, before pollen season hits.

Airborne Substances and Odors. Common asthma irritants include smoke from things like cigarettes or burning leaves. Pollution from smog, haze, and dust can also be dangerous for people with asthma. If you have asthma, you should stay away from someone who is fertilizing a lawn or spraying for insects—airborne fertilizers or pesticides can trigger asthma attacks. Fresh paint, room deodorizers, oven sprays, hair sprays, and perfume are also known to cause symptoms.

Exercise. For about 80 percent of people with asthma, physical activities like running, bicycling, or playing team sports can trigger symptoms. Doctors aren't sure why, but many believe it's because exercising causes you to breathe harder and more deeply, so you are breathing more allergens and airborne irritants into your lungs.

Secondhand smoke can be an asthma trigger.

Asthma in History

People have known about respiratory problems like asthma for a long time. A 1550 BCE document from ancient Egypt recommended a remedy of placing herbs on heated bricks and breathing in the fumes. At roughly the same time, the Chinese also recognized a problem they called "noisy breathing." A Chinese medical textbook from 1000 BCE prescribed the herb ma huang for asthma-like symptoms. Ma huang contains a chemical called ephedrine, a **stimulant** that opens airways. (Ephedrine would be brought to the West in modern times to help treat asthma.) The Greek physician Hippocrates is sometimes credited with discovering asthma as a specific condition in 460 BCE. The ancient Greeks called it *asqma*, which means to pant or breathe hard.

Doctors in the 1800s came to understand that asthma patients had muscle spasms in their bronchial airways, but even into the mid-1900s many believed the disease was caused by emotional distress. Research in 1966 disproved this theory and showed that people with asthma had a higher amount of allergy antibodies in their bloodstream. That proved people with asthma were more sensitive to their environment than others. In later decades, scientists discovered that allergens and other irritants could trigger asthma and that treating inflammation in bronchial airways could help control it.

Treating Asthma

There is no cure for asthma, but you can bring it under control by taking medicine and doing what you can to avoid your triggers. An asthma attack can be mild, with symptoms going away on their own. Or it can be a life-threatening event that sends you to the hospital. If you have asthma, there are two types of medicine your doctor may prescribe. The reason for the different types of medicine is they address two different problems that contribute to trouble breathing.

People with asthma often keep their inhalers nearby at all times, so that they are ready whenever symptoms arise.

- **Rescue inhaler**. One type of medicine is a fast-acting rescue medicine, taken from an inhaler, or "puffer." Fast-acting rescue inhalers help with asthma attacks. When you press the inhaler, it releases a gas-propelled mist. The mist contains a bronchodilator, a type of medicine that makes the muscles around the bronchial tubes relax and lets the airways open.
- **Controller medicine**. The other main type of treatment is called controller medicine. It's taken every day, either inhaled as a mist or swallowed as pills. Controller medicine helps manage long-term inflammation, making it less likely attacks will occur.

In addition to taking medicine, people with asthma should avoid irritants that trigger attacks. Pay attention when weather reports say that pollen counts are high or air quality is poor. That lets people with asthma know they should limit the time they spend outdoors. If you don't have local air-quality reports, you can find the information online at www.airnow.gov.

A GROWING PROBLEM

Asthma in the United States was on the rise for decades. But data from the U.S. National Health Interview Survey showed that, starting in 2013, the number of people with asthma had declined slightly. Cases of asthma are still growing for certain groups of people, though, including teens, people living in poverty, and those living in the South.

Worldwide, as many as 300 million people suffer from asthma, according to the World Health Organization. The disease is more common in developed countries. Overall, it has been on the rise for the past 40 years, as more communities have become urbanized and adopted modern lifestyles.

Who Gets Asthma?

Over 24 million people in the United States have asthma—approximately 1 in 12 children and 1 in 14 adults. The condition hits some groups of people harder than others. Researchers have some ideas about why that's so.

Genetics. Black children are twice as likely to get asthma as white children, and three times as likely to die from it, according to data from the CDC. That has made some researchers want to take a closer look at **genetics**. Most of the genetic information scientists have on asthma comes from studies of white populations, not blacks or other minorities. Researchers argue that more people from minority groups need to be included in asthma studies, in order to understand why certain ethnic groups are more prone to condition.

Poverty. Other researchers believe poverty is a bigger cause of differences in asthma rates. (It's possible that an income **disparity** may go hand-in-hand with the racial disparity.) Poverty means people are exposed more often to things that trigger asthma, like cockroaches in homes and air pollution and fumes in industrial neighborhoods. People might also have less money to repair water leaks that cause mold. They also may have less money to spend on health care. One study in New York City showed hospitalizations from asthma were as much as 16 times higher in zip codes where people were poor.

Air Pollution. Scientists have long believed that air pollution causes more people to have asthma. A 2016 study of asthma rates in Los Angeles, California, confirmed this link. Over two decades, pollution from cars and factories in Los Angeles dropped by about half. During the same time period, children with asthma showed a 32 percent drop in symptoms.

Some researchers say indoor air pollution from secondhand smoke, dust, and mold can be even more irritating than outdoor air pollution, because people spend most of their time indoors. Ironically, indoor air pollution may be getting worse, now that people are building homes to be more energy efficient.

Energy-efficient homes have **thermal** wraps around the framing. That lowers heating and cooling bills, but it also traps air—and indoor air pollution with it.

Asthma and Athletes

It might seem like a bad idea to exercise if you have asthma, since exercise can set off an attack. But in fact, doctors say they want people with asthma to continue to exercise as much as they can, because physical activity helps keep lungs healthy. There have even been some top U.S. athletes who have asthma.

Having asthma does not mean that you can't participate in sports.

Jackie Joyner-Kersee won six Olympic medals in track and field during the 1980s and 1990s. Diagnosed with asthma as a teen, Joyner-Kersee said that she learned to take her disease seriously after an asthma attack hospitalized her. She decided to get treatment, instead of trying to hide the problem from her coaches.

Kelsi Worrell, a record-breaking butterfly swimmer, got her asthma symptoms under control to earn a spot on the 2016 U.S. Olympic team. She swam in an early heat of the women's medley relay, and she received a gold medal after the team went on to win in the finals. Amazingly, one survey showed about a quarter of Olympic swimmers have asthma.

If you have asthma, ask your doctor about how to manage symptoms when you exercise. He may recommend you pretreat asthma by taking a puff from your inhaler before exercising. As long as the condition is well controlled, asthma doesn't have to keep you off the field.

Text-Dependent Questions

1. What are some common things that trigger asthma attacks?
2. What two types of medicine help people control asthma symptoms?
3. Why might poverty increase the number of people with asthma?

Research Project

How asthma-friendly is your school? Download *Managing Asthma: A Guide for Schools* from the National Heart, Lung, and Blood Institute's website at www.nhlbi.nih.gov/files/docs/resources/lung/asth_sch.pdf. Answer the questions on the page titled "How Asthma Friendly Is Your School?" Are there things your school could do to improve?

WORDS TO UNDERSTAND

carrier: someone who can give a disease or a gene to others, but who is not affected by it.

defective: imperfect or faulty.

duct: a tube in the body that carries a particular liquid.

enzymes: substances in the body that help chemical processes, such as digestion.

intravenous: entering the body through a vein.

recessive: a characteristic or condition that a child will have only if both of the child's parents have it.

regimen: a plan or set of rules for diet or exercise to make someone stay or become healthy.

CHAPTER THREE

Cystic Fibrosis

Cystic fibrosis (CF) is a rare disorder that affects both the lungs and the digestive system. CF causes the mucus in a person's body to become extra thick, which makes it difficult to breathe and also makes it harder to digest food.

A typical day for a kid with CF might go something like this: First, you probably have to get up at about 5 o'clock every morning because, like a runner training for competition, you go through a long health regimen. But it's not one that will win a race—instead, it's a regimen that keeps you alive. Every day, to keep your airways clear, you spend hours on chest therapy and breathing treatments, and you take dozens of pills. The treatments are time-consuming, expensive and, because there is currently no cure for CF, will continue your whole life. Fortunately, thanks to those treatments, you will be able to do things other people do, like go to school, play sports, marry, and have a career.

People of every ethnicity can have CF, but it occurs most often in white people whose ancestors came from northern Europe. Among whites, one in every 3,200 babies has CF. Without daily treatment, the extra-thick mucus

A nebulizer is a medical device that turns liquid medicine into tiny particles that can be breathed into the lungs. Nebulizers are important for people with CF and are used for a variety of other respiratory problems.

caused by the disease lingers in the lungs, making the person prone to life-threatening infections. Cystic fibrosis is called a "life-shortening" disease. People don't die from it, but their bodies often wear out from so many respiratory infections or from other problems the disease creates. Because of this, it's common for people with CF to die at a younger age than people who don't have the disease.

Understanding CF

Not much was known about cystic fibrosis before the 1930s, but doctors were describing its symptoms in sickly children as early as 1595. One children's folk song from Switzerland said, "The child will soon die whose brow tastes salty when kissed." And in fact, extra-salty skin is one of the ways cystic fibrosis is diagnosed, even today. It was first recognized as a disease in 1938, but it would be another 50 years before the gene responsible for cystic fibrosis was discovered.

One in every 31 persons in the United States carries the defective gene that causes cystic fibrosis. But not everyone who has the defective gene gets sick. Cystic fibrosis is a recessive disorder, which means both parents have to be CF carriers in order for their children be able to get the disease. If neither

THINGS TO KNOW ABOUT CYSTIC FIBROSIS

- 94 percent of people with cystic fibrosis are white.
- The average age of diagnosis is 2.
- The average person with CF has four to five respiratory infections per year and spends 20 days in the hospital because of them.

parent has CF but both are carriers, there's a one in four chance their baby will have cystic fibrosis.

The CF gene is responsible for making a protein that is found in the lining of respiratory airways and other places in the body, such as the intestines. The protein acts like a gateway: its job is to pass salt back and forth through the lining. Salt affects how much water will move to the surface of the lining. In a person with CF, there either aren't enough proteins or the proteins aren't working properly. That means there isn't enough water for the lining. As a result, the mucus becomes too thick.

This is big a problem for the respiratory system. Remember that in the lungs, the job of the mucus is to trap germs and other irritants. Then the cilia sweep those substances back up the airways to be coughed out. Normal mucus is thin and slippery. When mucus becomes too thick, as it is for people with cystic fibrosis, the cilia can't push it out. The mucus becomes stuck in the airways, where it traps even more germs and toxins, which can turn into serious infections. The mucus buildup can also plug airways, making it harder for someone with CF to breathe.

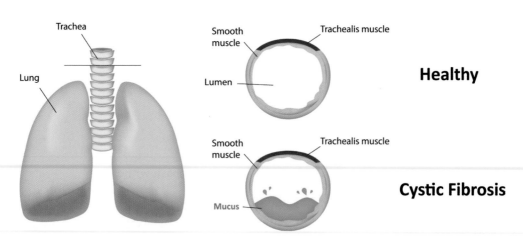

CF causes thick mucus to collect in the respiratory tract. This diagram shows the difference between the trachea of a healthy person and one who has CF.

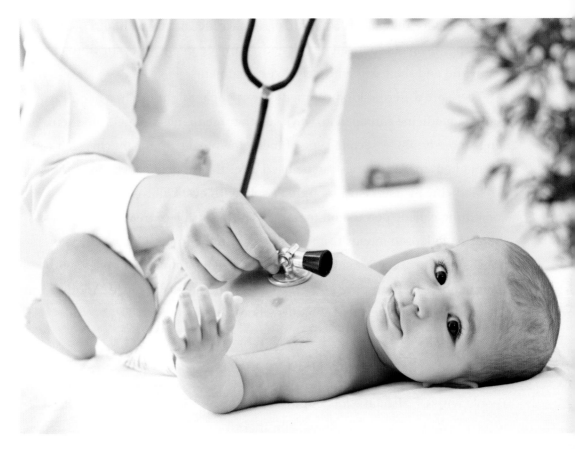

CF is usually diagnosed very early in life.

Parents often notice symptoms in their children with CF while they are still babies. They may wheeze and cough a lot, have more colds—even pneumonia—and their infections last longer. They may have severe diarrhea or constipation, and they gain weight more slowly than other children.

CF Treatments

People with cystic fibrosis must have lots of treatments every day to keep their bodies healthy. Most of these are to help them to breathe better.

One device they use is a nebulizer, a machine that turns liquid medicine into vapor droplets so it can be inhaled. Many people with cystic fibrosis begin and end their day with nebulizer treatments.

There are different kinds of medicines people might use in a nebulizer. Asthma medicine can open airways so other medicines can get into their lungs more easily. A second type of medicine breaks up the mucus, so it can be coughed up. Antibiotics can be used after that to help control infections.

Medicine by itself isn't enough. People with cystic fibrosis also get something called "percussion therapy." This is a type of treatment that uses vibration to loosen mucus from the airways in the lungs. One way this is done is by lying on your side and having someone thump your chest with their hands. The thumping and gravity help the mucus to move. Another way is to wear a special vest that vibrates when you plug it in.

Eating and CF

People with CF also take lots of pills, as many as 40 a day. One kind of pill helps them digest fats and proteins in their food. That's because cystic fibrosis interferes with the digestive system, too.

Thick mucus can plug the **ducts** in the pancreas. The pancreas is the part of the body that makes the **enzymes** that break down food in the digestive tract. Blocked ducts make it hard for the enzymes to go where they are needed. In people with CF, food passes through the body only partially digested. Because of this, people with CF tend to be undernourished, and many are thin and small for their age.

To help with digestion, people with CF take enzyme pills before every meal. They also try to eat more food to make up for nutrients that don't get absorbed. A person with CF might need to eat twice as many calories a day as someone who doesn't have the disease.

Infections and CF

EDUCATIONAL VIDEO

Scan this code for a video about kids living with CF.

Kids with CF will go to the hospital a lot compared to people without the disease. That's because germs that cause simple respiratory infections in a normal person can cause a life-threatening illness in a person with cystic fibrosis.

As people with CF get older, their lungs become damaged by repeated illnesses, and they eventually need more medical support to stay healthy. They might get a permanent tube, called a PICC line, inserted in their arm so they can easily be hooked up to intravenous antibiotics when they get sick. If their lungs become too damaged, they may need to breathe using an oxygen tank so they can get enough oxygen into their bodies. Eventually, their lungs are so damaged by infections that their body can't get enough oxygen. Or their body is poisoned by too much carbon dioxide.

Sometimes a person who is very ill gets one last chance at life. Doctors have been performing lung transplants since 1985. It's an operation that can be used for CF patients whose lungs are too damaged to support breathing much longer—usually, less than two years. There's a shortage of donated organs, however, so transplants are only granted to people who are very sick. Also, there are risks. Serious infections can result from the operation. Or, in a few cases, the body rejects the new organ, which means the body's defenses attack the organ as if it were a disease. The good news is that the new lungs won't have the damaged CF gene, so the mucus produced in them will be

People with CF are vulnerable to infections that can land them in the hospital.

normal. Other parts of the body will still have CF, though. More than half of people who get lung transplants are alive five years later.

Searching for a Cure

Doctors treat CF with medicines that thin mucus, reduce inflammation, and fight infection. But what if the root cause of CF could be fixed? There are two ways researchers are trying to do this:

- **Fix the protein.** One possibility is to fix the protein that regulates the salt on the surface of the airways. Two new drugs that do this were approved for sale in 2014 and 2015. Together, they could help over half the people with cystic fibrosis. But the medicine is expensive—it costs about $300,000 per year for each patient. And it won't cure everyone. There are lots of defects that can cause the CF gene to not work properly, and the new drugs only address two of them.

- **Fix the gene.** Another approach is to fix the defective gene that causes cystic fibrosis. When the CF gene was discovered in 1989, researchers became excited. They believed they could deliver healthy genes to the patient's cells to take over the work of the defective ones. Scientists tried getting the healthy genes into the body by attaching them to a virus. But the respiratory system's defenses blocked the virus. In 2015, researchers in England announced they had put healthy genes in a bubble of fat instead. When the treatment was tested, breathing improved by 4 percent in CF patients. That's not a lot, but it proves the idea could work. The researchers hope that by 2020, they'll be able to use gene therapy treat people with CF.

Text-Dependent Questions

1. How do people get cystic fibrosis? What group of people gets the disease the most?
2. What happens to your body when you have cystic fibrosis? What do you have to do to stay healthy?
3. Can cystic fibrosis be cured? Name two methods that are researchers hoping to use in the future.

Research Project

Two pages on the Cystic Fibrosis Foundation's website have timelines of advances made in understanding and treating CF: "Research Milestones" (www.cff.org/Our-Research/Our-Research-Approach/Research-Milestones) and "Our History" (www.cff.org/About-Us/About-the-Cystic-Fibrosis-Foundation/Our-History). Select the events you think are the most important and make your own timeline. What kind of pattern do you notice?

WORDS TO UNDERSTAND

latent: when a disease is present but does not produce symptoms.

mutate: when a living thing undergoes a permanent change in its genes.

pandemic: when a disease spreads very quickly and affects a large number of people over a wide area or throughout the world.

pulmonary: relating to the lungs.

susceptible: easily affected, influenced, or harmed by something.

CHAPTER FOUR

COPD and Respiratory Infections

Diseases like asthma and cystic fibrosis get a lot of attention—asthma because a lot of kids have it, and cystic fibrosis because researchers are narrowing in on a cure. But there are some other respiratory diseases that are also important.

COPD

Chronic obstructive **pulmonary** disorder (COPD) is a disease that makes it hard to breathe and saps the energy of people who have it. If you're reading this book, it's not likely you'll develop COPD any time soon, since it occurs mostly in people over the age of 40. But the decisions you make today could affect whether you get the disease in the future. The number one cause of COPD is long-term cigarette smoking—and 9 out of 10 people who smoke started when they were teenagers.

If you have a grandparent or another older relative with COPD, you've likely noticed the symptoms: a chronic, hacking cough, trouble carrying groceries,

COPD in older people is associated with a lifetime of smoking, although that is not the only cause.

or difficulty climbing the stairs. As symptoms get worse over time, even basic activities like walking can become extremely difficult. COPD is the third leading cause of death in the United States, according to the CDC. And it is on the rise as the world's population ages.

COPD is an umbrella term for several diseases that cause irreversible damage to your lungs, including chronic bronchitis and emphysema. Chronic bronchitis comes from many years of irritating the bronchial tubes with things like cigarette smoke. Your airways become permanently scarred and extra mucus is produced all the time. That makes you cough a lot, and it causes frequent infections.

While chronic bronchitis affects airways, emphysema affects the alveoli, the tiny air sacs at the end of the airways. In healthy lungs, the air sacs are like little balloons, filling up and deflating as you breathe in and out. With emphysema, the air sacs lose their elastic quality, and the walls between many of the air sacs may be destroyed. Remember, the alveoli are where oxygen from the air enters your bloodstream. Damaging them means less oxygen gets into your body.

COPD has no cure yet, and it is not known whether damage to the lungs can be reversed. The body creates new air sacs until you are about 20 years old, but growth stops after that. The good news is that getting treatment can slow down the progress of COPD. Doctors recommend people with the disease quit smoking immediately and improve their energy levels with healthy eating and exercise. To help with breathing problems, doctors may prescribe medicines to open airways and control inflammation. Severe cases of COPD may call for oxygen therapy and even lung transplants.

EDUCATIONAL VIDEO

Scan this code for a video about what it's like to have COPD.

LIVE LONG AND PROSPER

The actor Leonard Nimoy, who played Dr. Spock on *Star Trek*, died of COPD in 2015, at the age of 83. Nimoy played a half-human, half-alien science officer aboard the Starship *Enterprise* in the original TV series and in a number of movies that followed. In 2014 he announced he had been diagnosed with COPD, even though he had given up cigarettes 30 years earlier. "Not soon enough," the actor tweeted to his fans.

After Nimoy's death, the actor Zachary Quinto, who played a young Spock in more recent *Star Trek* movies, said, "My heart is broken. I love you profoundly my dear friend, and I will miss you every day."

Respiratory Infections

The numbers of people who have been diagnosed with asthma, cystic fibrosis, and COPD have been on the rise in recent decades. But the story of respiratory disease has not always been one of rising numbers. Many serious diseases have been brought under control over the past 100 years by medicines, vaccines, and healthier lifestyles. You have probably had a pertussis (whooping cough) vaccination or a tuberculosis skin test. Perhaps you get a flu shot every year. These precautions are a big reason you don't hear much about people dying of these diseases today.

Respiratory infections are caused by germs that settle in your airways and lungs and attack healthy cells. They cause symptoms like congestion, a runny nose, cough, fatigue, and fever. People treat infections with bed rest, fluids, and medicines. It's not a good idea to ignore even a simple infection, like a cold or flu, because it can spread to the entire respiratory system and make you susceptible to more serious illnesses.

Pneumonia. Pneumonia can feel a lot like the flu. Both come with high fevers and both make you feel wiped out. But pneumonia is a more serious disease that can lead to hospitalization and, occasionally, even death. Besides the flu-like symptoms, people with pneumonia often have severe chest pains and trouble breathing.

A cold or the flu is an infection of the airways. Pneumonia, on the other hand, infects the alveoli. The tiny air sacs in the lungs become inflamed and they fill up with fluid. Doctors can see the fluid in a chest X-ray. The fluid gets in the way of oxygen moving into the bloodstream, which is why pneumonia makes breathing difficult. Many times pneumonia can be treated at home by taking antibiotics, but serious cases require hospitalization.

Tuberculosis. Tuberculosis has been called the forgotten plague. By the beginning of the 19th century, it had killed 1 in 7 of all people who had ever lived. Victims suffered from hacking, bloody coughs, pain in their lungs, and fatigue. The disease was also called "consumption," because it seemed to consume its victims. They got thinner and thinner, and it seemed like they coughed themselves to death.

Tuberculosis is caused by a type of bacteria that can be carried in the dust or air. It is contagious and can be passed on by a cough or sneeze. A person can be infected without developing the disease. Someone might carry the latent infection in his or her body for years before becoming sick. Only people with active tuberculosis are contagious, however.

In 1944, researchers developed the first medicine to treat active tuberculosis. Today, doctors prescribe a mix of several medicines, taken for 6 to 9 months, for people with TB. It's very important for people with the disease to finish taking all of the medicines, exactly as they are prescribed. If they don't, the TB bacteria

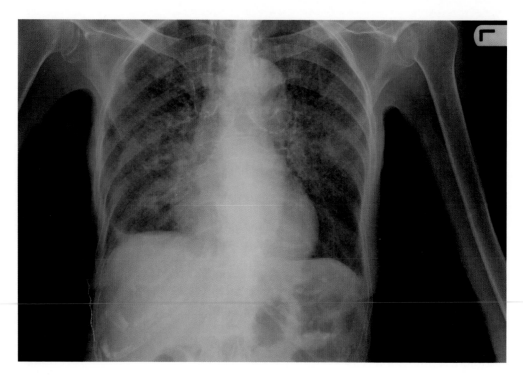

An X-ray of lungs infected with tuberculosis.

that are still alive in their bodies may become resistant to the drugs. Drug-resistant TB is harder and more expensive to treat.

Doctors today also give people a skin test to see if the bacteria is in their body. People who test positive for this latent TB must get treatment, too.

In the United States today, only 3 people in 100,000 get tuberculosis, according to the CDC. But worldwide, the disease remains a much bigger problem. Tuberculosis is one of the top 10 causes of death in poor and lower-middle-income countries, according to the World Health Organization.

Whooping Cough. Pertussis, also called whooping cough, is another disease that was once widespread. Today, you may only know of it because you got a pertussis vaccination when you were little. Before there was a vaccine, about 200,000 children in the United States got sick with the disease each year, and about 9,000 died.

Whooping cough is a highly contagious infection. The disease starts like a cold, but after 2 weeks, patients start having violent coughing fits. After a fit, they gasp for air. and when they breathe in it resembles a "whoop" sound. The coughing may last for 10 or more weeks. Because of this, it has also been called the "100-day cough."

American doctors thought they had beaten whooping cough when a vaccine for it became widely available in the 1940s. By the 1970s, fewer than 3,000 people per year got the disease. But the number is now slowly rising again. In recent years, outbreaks of whooping cough have been reported in parts of California, Washington, New Hampshire, Vermont, Ohio, Pennsylvania, and other states. In 2014 over 32,000, people in the United States got the disease.

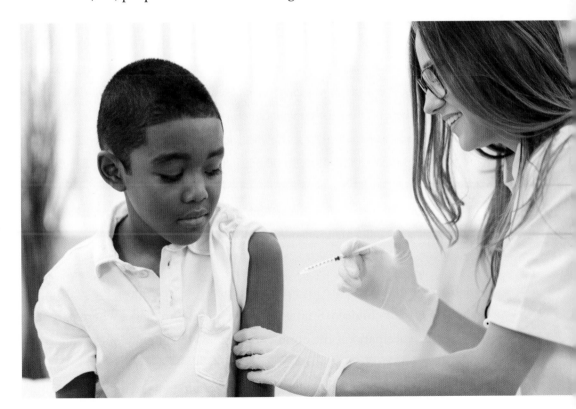

The vaccine against pertussis (whooping cough) is effective; unfortunately, as rates of vaccination have gone down, rates of illness and even death from pertussis have gone up.

A DEADLY FLU

In 1918 a flu pandemic killed at least 30 million people worldwide, three times the number of soldiers killed in World War I. In the United States, more than half a million people died, some in as little as a single day. Flu is caused by the influenza virus. It is spread by coughing or by contact with someone's hand or an infected surface. But in 1918, doctors were not certain how it started or how to stop it.

"People were left very weak with it, on account of the high fever," said one woman who was 10 at the time. "All the schools and public places, every place was closed for at least nearly 2 or 3 weeks."

The first flu vaccine was developed in 1944. Because the influenza virus mutates, the vaccine is updated every year. That's why people get a yearly flu shot, instead of just a one-time vaccine.

Pictured above: the Red Cross Ambulance Station in Washington, DC, during the influenza pandemic of 1918.

One reason is that there are groups of parents who are opposed to getting vaccinations for their children. Studies have shown that in places where parents opted out of the vaccinations, the number of people who got whooping cough was higher—in one study, it was more than double.

Another reason is people may not be getting vaccinated enough. The original whooping cough vaccine was replaced in the 1990s by a new type that has fewer side effects. That's good, but the new vaccine wears off more quickly. So it's very

1

important for people to get all of the recommended shots. People should get five pertussis shots by they time they are 6 years old, a pertussis booster as an adolescent, and another booster as an adult, according to the CDC.

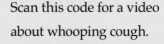

EDUCATIONAL VIDEO

Scan this code for a video about whooping cough.

Text-Dependent Questions

1. Who gets COPD, and why does it matter to teens?
2. How does pneumonia make it hard to breathe?
3. Is it possible that a person who isn't sick with tuberculosis would still need treatment? Why?
4. Why does whooping cough have that name?

Research Project

Some things that contribute to respiratory problems are difficult or even impossible to control. But others, like smoking and pollution can be addressed—sometimes by individuals and sometimes by society as a whole. What do you think are the most important things people should do to reduce the number of people with respiratory problems? Make a list and put your suggestions in order, starting with the ones you think would be the most effective, and ending with those that are the least effective. Look for news articles about asthma, pollution, smoking, indoor air quality, poverty, obesity, and global warming to help you decide.

WORDS TO UNDERSTAND

cardiovascular: relating to the heart; describes exercise that causes the heart to beat faster and harder, such as running.

dander: tiny flecks of skin shed by animals with fur or feathers.

spore: a cell made by some plants that is like a seed and can produce a new plant.

CHAPTER FIVE

Living with Respiratory Disease

I f you have a chronic respiratory disease, how well you feel will often be tied to how well you are breathing. Medicines and therapy will help to manage your symptoms. Beyond these, there are other choices you can make to feel as healthy as possible.

For Everyone

All people, whether they have a respiratory disease or not, can help their lungs in a number of ways. Here are some things you can do:

- **Don't smoke.** Cigarette smoke causes swelling in your airways and makes them narrower. It also destroys your lung tissue. Both of these things make it harder to breathe.
- **Avoid pollutants when possible.** Secondhand smoke, outdoor air pollution, and chemicals in the home are all things that can hurt your

Exercise helps strengthen your lungs.

lungs. Avoid outdoor exercise on days when smog is bad. If you can, stay away from people who are smoking.

- **Get regular exercise.** Cardiovascular exercise, like soccer, bicycling, or running, helps to make your lungs stronger.
- **Wash your hands often.** This will reduce the number of colds or other respiratory infections you get. Use soap and water when you wash. Use alcohol-based hand sanitizers, like Germ-X or Purell, if you cannot use soap and water.

If You Have Asthma

If you have asthma, it's important that you understand what your triggers are and learn to avoid them as much as possible. That can be easier to say than do—

sometimes it may seem like triggers are everywhere. Here are some suggestions for different triggers:

- **Pets.** Keep pets with fur out of your home. If you must have a pet, choose one with less dander and keep it out of your bedroom.

- **Dust mites.** Ask your parents if you can get special dust-proof covers for your mattress and pillow. Stay out of rooms while they are being vacuumed.

- **Cockroaches.** Make sure your put food away in sealed containers. Never leave food, dirty dishes, or standing water out.

- **Pollen and outdoor mold.** Keep windows closed during allergy season. Try to stay indoors from late morning to afternoon, when pollen and mold spore counts are highest. If you do go outside, change your clothes when you get home.

- **Tobacco smoke.** Ask your parents to not let people smoke in your family's home or car.

A peak flow meter can tell you if you have asthma symptoms even before you can feel them. That can ward off a dangerous asthma attack. A peak flow meter is a handheld gauge that measures how fast you are able to blast air out of your lungs. When your asthma flares up, you will not be able to blast as much air as you normally can.

Your doctor should give you an "asthma action plan" that tells you what to do if you get a low reading. The plan will tell you what signs show that your asthma is getting worse, and it will tell you how to adjust your medicines when you see these signs. It will also let you know when to seek emergency care.

EDUCATIONAL VIDEO

Scan this QR code for more tips on living with asthma.

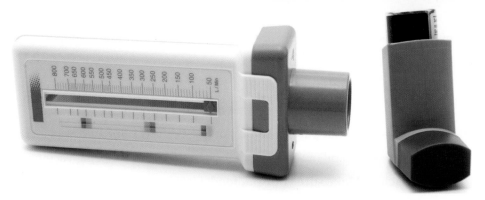

Two important tools for people with asthma: a peak flow meter and an inhaler.

If You Have Cystic Fibrosis

If you have cystic fibrosis (CF), keeping yourself healthy is a big job. Here's how to deal with various challenges you may face:

- **Time mangement.** Between dozens of medicines and airway clearance therapy, it may feel like there aren't enough hours in the day to get everything done. Develop a routine that makes treatments a normal part of the day. Make a list of everything that's important in your life relating to health, family, school, friends, and hobbies. Rank the items by priority. Then create a schedule that makes time for the top things on your list. Talk to other people in your life about the schedule to help reinforce it.
- **Diet.** You can add proteins and fats to your diet by drinking protein shakes, nutrition drinks, or smoothies. Try fast and easy snacks and meals, such as microwave breakfasts and sandwiches, cheese and cracker snacks, granola or protein bars, pudding snacks, nuts, and sunflower seeds.
- **Staying healthy.** Your parents should tell your teachers and school administrators that you have CF, in case you need accommodations. You may need time at school for airway clearance therapy or extra time during lunch to get your enzyme pills from the nurse's office. You may need more frequent access to drinking water and the bathroom. You will

54

likely need a plan to get homework, and maybe tutoring, if you miss classes. Make sure you know how your school will help you.

- **Exercise.** Exercise strengthens your lungs and helps to clear out mucus. If you are able, you should exercise for 30 minutes a day, 3 times a week. People with CF lose more salt when they sweat. So besides drinking water, you should eat a salty snack, like pretzels, before or after you exercise.
- **Illness.** Listen to your body. Pay attention when symptoms like coughing are "off" from what is normal for you. Also pay attention to how energetic you feel or whether you have less appetite. These may be early signs of a lung infection. Ask your parents if you can see a doctor if these occur.

Being a Friend

If you know someone with a respiratory illness, you'll probably want to be supportive. Here are ways you can help:

TELLING FRIENDS ABOUT CF

It can be hard to tell your friends you have CF. But, eventually, they may need to know, in order to understand and accommodate the things you do to stay healthy. Stick with the facts and keep it simple. Say something like, "I have a health condition called CF. I have to spend time every day getting breathing treatments. I also take medicine so I can digest my food better." Always remember that CF is something you have, but it is not the entirety of who you are.

- **Do not expose their family to illness.** Wash your hands when you enter their home, and if someone in your family is ill, do not visit. Get yearly flu shots.
- **Don't smoke.** Secondhand smoke is bad for everyone, but for people with a respiratory disease, it can make a challenging situation even worse.
- **Be sensitive to the types of stories you share.** Think carefully before sharing a dramatic story, such as one about someone who died of the disease. Also, be careful when talking about treatments for diseases that have no known cure. Don't assume that your friend can just fix the problem easily.
- **Remember that people with respiratory disease are still people.** Treat your friend the same way you would any other friend. Be sensitive to his or her unique needs and concerns, but don't treat your friend like a freak, either. Everyone wants to feel normal.

Text-Dependent Questions

1. What are three things a person with asthma might do to avoid triggers?
2. How does exercise help your lungs? How does it especially help people with CF?
3. What are two things you should *not* do if you are around a friend with a respiratory disease?

Research Project

Using tips from this chapter and additional ones you find in your own research, create a pamphlet that gives advice to people with respiratory conditions, their families, and their friends. What should people with these conditions do to improve their health? What can families and friends do to help? (You can start with the "Further Reading" section to find more suggestions.)

FURTHER READING

Felner, Kevin. *COPD for Dummies.* Hoboken, NJ: Wiley, 2008.

Johns Hopkins Cystic Fibrosis Center. "Teen Zone." http://www.hopkinscf.org/teen-zone.

National Heart, Lung, and Blood Institute. "So You Have Asthma: A Guide for Patients and Their Families." http://catalog.nhlbi.nih.gov/catalog/product/So-You-Have-Asthma-A-Guide-for-Patients-and-Their-Families/13-5248.

National Heart, Lung, and Blood Institute. "What Is COPD." http://www.nhlbi.nih.gov/health/health-topics/topics/copd/names.

TeensHealth. "Lungs and Respiratory System." http://kidshealth.org/en/teens/lungs.html.

Zuchora-Walske, Christine. *Living With Asthma.* Edina, MN: ABDO Publishing, 2014.

Educational Videos

Chapter One: Classroom Video. "The Respiratory System." https://youtu.be/hc1YtXc_84A.

Chapter Two: National Asthma Campaign. "What Causes Asthma?" https://youtu.be/K4fKkfVnzY4.

Chapter Three: CFF—Greater Illinois Chapter. "2015 Cystic Fibrosis Foundation Video." https://youtu.be/DySt5tLi4G8.

Chapter Four: Novartis. "COPD Patients and Everyday Activities." https://youtu.be/jysE5h8_2FE.

Chapter Four: Mayo Clinic. "Whooping Cough." https://youtu.be/l5SHtdczSBc.

Chapter Five: Seattle Childrens. "Living with Asthma." https://youtu.be/0nQr-tsRiB4.

SERIES GLOSSARY

accommodation: an arrangement or adjustment to a new situation; for example, schools make accommodations to help students cope with illness.

anemia: an illness caused by a lack of red blood cells.

autoimmune: type of disorder where the body's immune system attacks the body's tissues instead of germs.

benign: not harmful.

biofeedback: a technique used to teach someone how to control some bodily functions.

capillaries: tiny blood vessels that carry blood from larger blood vessels to body tissues.

carcinogens: substances that can cause cancer to develop.

cerebellum: the back part of the brain; it controls movement.

cerebrum: the front part of the brain; it controls many higher-level thinking and functions.

cholesterol: a waxy substance associated with fats that coats the inside of blood vessels, causing cardiovascular disease.

cognitive: related to conscious mental activities, such as learning and thinking.

communicable: transferable from one person to another.

congenital: a condition or disorder that exists from birth.

correlation: a connection between different things that suggests they may have something to do with one another.

dominant: in genetics, a dominant trait is expressed in a child even when the trait is only inherited from one parent.

environmental factors: anything that affects how people live, develop, or grow. Climate, diet, and pollution are examples.

genes: units of hereditary information.

hemorrhage: bleeding from a broken blood vessel.

hormones: substances the body produces to instruct cells and tissues to perform certain actions.

inflammation: redness, swelling, and tenderness in a part of the body in response to infection or injury.

insulin: a hormone produced in the pancreas that controls cells' ability to absorb glucose.

lymphatic system: part of the human immune system; transports white blood cells around the body.

malignant: harmful; relating to tumors, likely to spread.

mutation: a change in the structure of a gene; some mutations are harmless, but others may cause disease.

neurological: relating to the nervous system (including the brain and spinal cord).

neurons: specialized cells found in the central nervous system (the brain and spinal cord).

occupational therapy: a type of therapy that teaches one how to accomplish tasks and activities in daily life.

oncology: the study of cancer.

orthopedic: dealing with deformities in bones or muscles.

prevalence: how common or uncommon a disease is in any given population.

prognosis: the forecast for the course of a disease that predicts whether a person with the disease will get sicker, recover, or stay the same.

progressive disease: a disease that generally gets worse as time goes on.

psychomotor: relating to movement or muscle activity resulting from mental activity.

recessive: in genetics, a recessive trait will only be expressed if a child inherits it from both parents.

remission: an improvement in or disappearance of someone's symptoms of disease; unlike a cure, remission is usually temporary.

resilience: the ability to bounce back from difficult situations.

seizure: an event caused by unusual brain activity resulting in physical or behavior changes.

syndrome: a condition with a set of associated symptoms.

ulcers: a break or sore in skin or tissue where cells disintegrate and die. Infections may occur at the site of an ulcer.

INDEX

Illlustrations are indicated by page numbers in *italic* type.

ABOUT THE ADVISOR

Heather Pelletier, Ph.D., is a pediatric staff psychologist at Rhode Island Hospital/Hasbro Children's Hospital with a joint appointment as a clinical assistant professor in the departments of Psychiatry and Human Behavior and Pediatrics at the Warren Alpert Medical School of Brown University. She is also the director of behavioral pain medicine in the division of Children's Integrative therapies, Pain management and Supportive care (CHIPS) in the department of Pediatrics at Hasbro Children's Hospital. Dr. Pelletier provides clinical services to children in various medical specialty clinics at Hasbro Children's Hospital, including the pediatric gastroenterology, nutrition, and liver disease clinics.

ABOUT THE AUTHOR

Carole Hawkins is a freelance writer who has worked for top news outlets in Georgia and Northeast Florida covering politics, business, the arts, history and science. She has received writing awards from the Florida Press Club, Georgia Associated Press and the National Association of Real Estate Editors. An education enthusiast, she trained as a Montessori teacher through the Seton Montessori Institute.

PHOTO CREDITS